Contents

Words included in the glossary are in **bold** the first time they appear in each chapter.

The Native Americans

The Native North American people have produced some of the world's greatest art — fantastic masks, feathered headdresses, intricate carvings. These works of art are fascinating in themselves, but they are also part of a larger story. They tell us about the lives and cultures of the people who lived in North America, what they considered beautiful, what they feared and hated, and how they prospered or declined.

Different lifestyle

The most widely held theory is that the story begins thousands of years ago, when people first passed across the Bering Strait from Asia into North America. By the 15th century, when white explorers first arrived in North America, there was a wide variety of native cultures. In the southwest, Native Americans had built small cities of **adobe** brick, called **pueblos**; in the forests of the northeast, there was a sophisticated alliance of tribes; on the **Plains**, in the middle of the continent, **nomadic** people lived in **tepees** and hunted herds of buffalo.

Many of the first meetings between Europeans and Native Americans were friendly, but the peace did not last. Through the 1600s, 1700s and 1800s, white **settlers** steadily pushed west. Tribes lost many of their people through European diseases. Some Native Americans tried to resist the whites but were crushed in bloody wars. Others signed treaties, not understanding that a piece of paper could change ownership of the land. By the late 1800s, Native American survivors had been forced on to **reservations**, where they were expected to live like whites.

▼ An Iroquois mask. Every mask was different, though they followed the same general design. A person carved a mask after having a vision. Once he had the vision, he could join the Masked Medicine Society. The society performed rituals that were intended to cure disease.

Like most Iroquois masks, it is painted in black and red, to make it more dramatic

Mask is made from wood and horse hair

Ideas about Native Americans

During the period of settlement, many whites portrayed Native Americans as bloody and ruthless – red-skinned savages with strange beliefs and customs. It was mostly after the Native American peoples ceased to be a threat that whites became aware of their extraordinary culture. The Native Americans had largely oral cultures in which their knowledge, history and stories were passed on by word of mouth, not writing. They left few documents behind. Their works of art, however, are fascinating objects of skill, delicacy and great beauty. They prove that the crude stereotypes of brutal savages were wrong. Instead, their art reveals a different way of seeing the world.

◄ This young Sioux woman, photographed in about 1907, wears an elaborate outfit, most likely for a special occasion. Her beads are made from porcupine quills or glass. Plains Native Americans often traded with white settlers for glass beads. The designs would identify her tribe.

Clothing is made from buffalo or deer skin, softened through a tanning process

Beads are most likely from flattened porcupine quills, or glass

Art that serves a function

Native Americans did not practise art for art's sake alone. With great skill they created works of beauty, but the things they made mostly had important uses. The carved masks made by the Kwakiutl, the colourful patterns of Navajo blankets, the painted figures on Lakota robes, all served a function. Some had a practical use, but others had a more spiritual significance: they showed rank, evoked magical powers, or ensured a successful crop or hunt. Most importantly, Native American art demonstrated a view of the world in which almost everything in nature – from the soaring eagle to the grasses of the earth – was sacred.

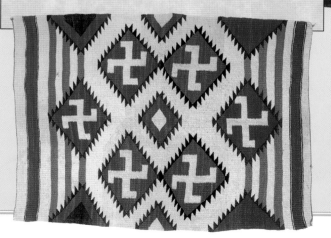

◄ The design on this Navajo rug represents the 'rolling log' myth, of a man who is cast out by his tribe and rides a hollow log down a river. He is helped by spirits to land in a new, bountiful place. To the Navajo, the symbol represents friendship and good will.

Art as evidence

Each piece of Native American art fits into the larger history of the Native American people. The art can show where they settled, their surroundings, and whether they lived in one place or moved about frequently. It reveals their religious beliefs and what they held sacred. It might record a significant event, or be a sign of great change.

A culture in movement

Native Americans who lived on the vast, grassy, open Plains moved frequently to follow **game**. Their artwork – painted buffalo skins and beadwork on clothing – demonstrates to us that their culture was nomadic. Clothing and buffalo robes were easily wrapped up and carried across large spaces.

The hide is designed with four sections. The number four was important. It represented four directions (north, south, east, west) and the four seasons

Buffalo robes told stories. This panel could be of the artist's meeting with mythical figures or ancestors

A culture in place

In the southwest, Native Americans lived in adobe brick villages, called pueblos. Their way of life depended on farming. Much of their artwork was related to the seasonal pattern of planting, growing and harvesting. Beautiful, colourful masks and ceremonial dress were used at special times of the year in **rituals** that ensured a healthy crop for the village. Farming also gave the cultures a steady supply of food and a sense of security. They created expert objects of craftsmanship, such as weaving and pottery.

◀ Native Americans covered buffalo robes with highly personal designs. This robe was probably created by a female artist. Male artists tended to be less abstract.

The circle was an important symbol. It represented the belief that life was a cycle without a beginning or an end

Southwestern art continues to flourish today, and that fact also tells a story. The people who lived in the pueblos were able to overcome the shock of meeting Europeans. They managed to keep their communities and their culture mostly intact. Today, they continue to produce artwork that combines their ancient traditions with the perspectives and techniques of the modern world.

An incomplete story

Even the absence of art can tell a story. Many of the eastern tribes, especially the ones that were the first to come into contact with European settlers, were destroyed or forced to leave their land, and their cultures largely disappeared with them. Their art was created from animal skin and wood, materials that deteriorate quickly in the moist eastern climate, and few items have survived.

Some art tells incomplete stories. In central North America, several ancient Native American civilizations flourished and then disappeared. We have only silent giant mounds and stone **artefacts** to examine. They are evidence of a sophisticated and strong culture, but we do not know many details about the people's beliefs or how they lived.

▶ Sioux moccasins. Shoes of this quality would be worn on special occasions and during ceremonies.

Softened porcupine quills are stitched to make this design

Art or craft?

Native Americans, like people all over the world, decorated common objects such as tools, baskets and clothing. These objects are often very beautiful, but some experts argue that they are not art. Art, they say, occurs when craft and inspiration (usually religious) meet – such as in masks, sand paintings, or in the designs an individual painted on his shield.

▶ This Tlingit dagger from the late 19th century has a copper blade and a carved and inlaid haft (handle) representing a mythical bear.

These abstract designs were unique to each tribe. The craftsman could take small liberties with each design

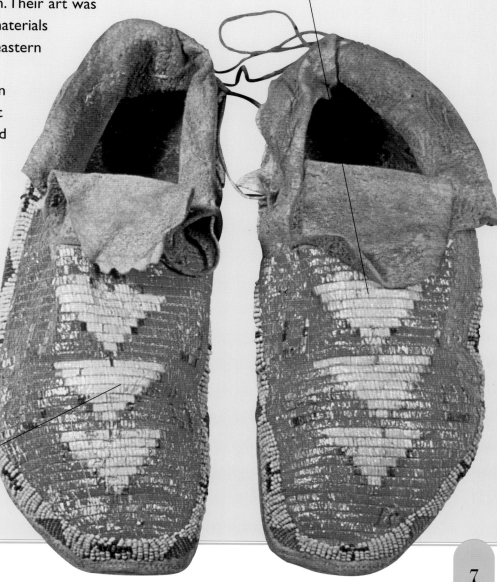

7

A chronological history

The most commonly held theory is that people first came to North America from Asia at least 12,000 years ago. The climate was colder then, and vast sheets of ice covered most of Canada and the northern USA. With billions of litres of water frozen, the ocean level fell and uncovered a stretch of land between Asia and North America. This strip of land, located across the Bering Strait between Alaska and eastern Asia, became a bridge for people to migrate to North America. **Settlers** may have also travelled over the ocean, either across the Bering Strait or further down the coast, in canoes or larger boats. This theory has never been proved, however, and it may be that people existed in the Americas long before they existed in Europe or Asia.

Ancient **artefacts** have been found scattered throughout the Americas, from Canada to Peru. Scientific tests of these artefacts provide a wide range of dates for the earliest people, from 20,000 BC to 38,000 BC. Some scholars believe there were people living in the Americas even further back in time, possibly as early as 60,000 BC.

▼ This map shows the regions originally inhabited by Native Americans, and significant places mentioned in the text.

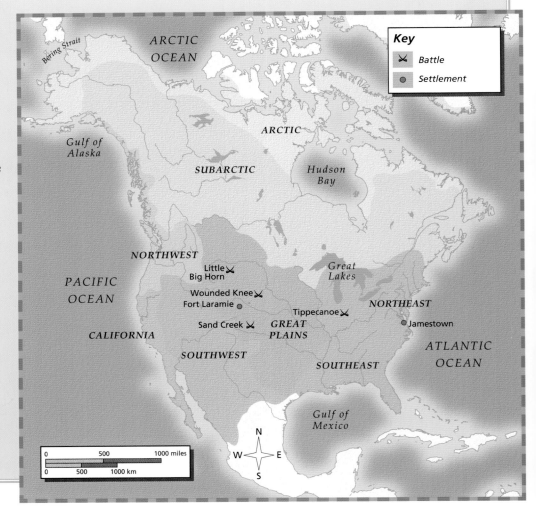

Key

⚔ Battle

● Settlement

ARCTIC OCEAN

Bering Strait

ARCTIC

Gulf of Alaska

SUBARCTIC

Hudson Bay

NORTHWEST

Great Lakes

PACIFIC OCEAN

Little Big Horn ⚔

Wounded Knee ⚔

Fort Laramie ●

Tippecanoe ⚔

NORTHEAST

● Jamestown

Sand Creek ⚔

GREAT PLAINS

CALIFORNIA

ATLANTIC OCEAN

SOUTHWEST

SOUTHEAST

Gulf of Mexico

0   500   1000 miles
0   500   1000 km

N
W   E
S

Common traits

The Native Americans developed separate societies, with their own languages and customs. Their lives did, however, share common features, and one of these was the food they ate. Native Americans first lived on a diet of meat, nuts, roots and berries. Archaeologists have found ancient woven baskets, which were used to collect and store food.

People came to discover that they could plant certain seeds and harvest the fruit or grain regularly each season. This provided a reliable supply of food and meant that they no longer had to wander in search of animals to hunt. They began to stay in one place. Farming was practised in many areas of North America. In the northeast, people cleared patches of forest and grew crops. They remained in the area for years. When the soil was worn out, they moved on.

The Native Americans probably came to North America in several waves. From 5000 to 1000 BC the Native Americans developed sophisticated methods of hunting large animals. In the Great Lakes region people fashioned objects from copper. After 1000 BC, the Native American people began to develop complex civilizations, in some places with enormous buildings and centralized rule.

▶ Spears from c.700–1200, which once belonged to Anasazi people living in the southwest. The Native Americans were skilful hunters of large game, including deer, moose and buffalo.

Hunting rituals

This tiny figure of a deer, made from split twigs and bark, was found in a cave in the Grand Canyon and is one of the earliest examples of North American art on display today. It was probably used in a hunting **ritual**, to try to guarantee the presence of game and give the hunters the luck and skill needed to spear it. It illustrates how important hunting was to the first Native Americans, who had not yet learned to farm.

Hunting

Much of the earliest Native American artwork relates to hunting. One tribe had a type of spear with what they called an *atlatl* shaft, which provided more power and accuracy for the thrower. Part of the *atlatl* was made of stone and was often carved into animal shapes.

Spear points made from carefully chipped stone

Animal tendons bind the spear points to the shaft

9

The pueblos

In the dry and **arid** southwest, Native Americans originally lived **nomadic** lives, sheltering mostly in caves. Families gradually came together in villages and established simple farms, and these flowered into civilizations. One of the first recognizable cultures in the American southwest was the Mogollon, which means 'mountain people'.

The first pueblos

Mogollon architecture shows a development from nomadic hunter-gatherers to farmers. The first settlers in the region hunted animals with spears. They also gathered nuts and berries to eat.

When the Native Americans began to plant corn and farm the land, the wandering lifestyle largely ended. The Mogollon built structures – large covered pits – to store the corn they harvested. Later the Mogollon began to cover these pits with timber, and used them as homes. Previously they had lived in caves and temporary structures. Around the 7th century, the Mogollon began to live above ground in houses built of **adobe** bricks and stone. Then **clans** – formed by a mother, her married daughters and their families – began joining their houses together. They formed a giant, single structure that encompassed the entire village – the first **pueblo**.

▼ Cliff Palace, Colorado. Exactly why southwestern Native Americans began building defensive stone villages in cliffs is unknown.

Large tower is still intact. It may have been built to help protect the village

Ruins of several houses

***Kiva** chamber. This would have been covered with a wooden roof*

▶ A Mogollon bowl from the early 14th century.

Hohokum culture

The Mogollon culture influenced two other southwestern groups – the Anasazi and the Hohokum. The Hohokum people flourished between AD 600 and 1400. They left behind painted pottery and dolls. Designs etched on sea shells have been found that date from AD 1000 – among the first examples of etching in world history. To water their thirsty crops, the Hohokum dug hundreds of kilometres of irrigation ditches.

Development of pueblos

The large pueblos were abandoned around 1300. It is thought a devastating drought, or perhaps invaders, forced their inhabitants to leave them. Some scholars believe internal disagreements and rebellion caused them to break up. Later pueblos were constructed in the giant seams in cliff faces. Others were built in the cool shadows of massive rock formations. These pueblos were built as strongholds during a period of growing unrest and insecurity.

The artist used a geometric pattern that was several hundred years old

Patterns were originally copied from designs woven into baskets

Mogollon pottery

The Mogollon culture is remembered largely for its stunning examples of painted pottery. They were decorated in black and white, with geometric patterns, animals and people. Many of the samples recovered from graves have a hole punched in the bottom, a sign of a ritual to release the soul in the pottery. Many Native American cultures believed each object was inhabited by a spirit.

Anasazi

North of the Hohokum lived the Anasazi. The Anasazi were skilled basketmakers who wove brilliant designs. They grew cotton and made cotton cloth, which they decorated with patterns still used today. The descendants of the Anasazi built larger and larger pueblo communities. One pueblo, built about 1000 years ago, covered more than a hectare and housed more than 1000 people – a world record size for an 'apartment building' that was only broken in New York City in 1882.

◀ This woven basket shows a typical black and red pattern used by Anasazi craftsmen. Baskets were essential to carry food and store goods, especially before the Anasazi began using pottery around AD 300.

First contacts

On 12 October 1492, three Spanish ships led by an Italian sailor named Christopher Columbus spotted an island off the coast of North America. At first Columbus thought he had found the Spice Islands to the east of India, known as the Indies. He named the startled inhabitants of the islands 'Indians'. 'So peaceful are these people, that swear to your Majesties there is no better nation on Earth,' Columbus wrote to the king and queen of Spain. 'They love their neighbours as themselves, and their discourse is ever sweet and gentle.' Scholars estimate that when Columbus stumbled across the continent there were several million Native Americans living there. They spoke hundreds of different languages. By the late 1800s, the population had been reduced to 228,000 and nearly half the languages were **extinct**.

Disease and war

The main reason for the terrible death toll amongst Native Americans in the 17th century was disease. European settlers following Columbus carried diseases that the Native American population had no resistance to. **Smallpox**, influenza and measles wiped out entire villages. Hundreds of thousands, possibly millions, died.

▼ An idealized view of a meeting between Europeans and Native Americans, created by a European artist.

The chiefs are shown as carrying peace pipes, a sign that the meeting would lead to signing a treaty

On the other hand, a Native American is also shown carrying a tomahawk, a symbol of imminent war

In 1607, a group of about 110 Englishmen established a colony on the coast of Virginia. The group soon faced starvation, but a local Native American named Squanto helped teach the English to plant corn and to fish. However, he received little recognition for this. In 1614, Squanto was captured by the English and sold into slavery. He worked in a monastery for three years and then managed to escape. When he returned to his village in 1619, he found it had vanished. The inhabitants had either fled or been killed by disease.

The Native Americans were also killed in war. By 1622, an Algonquian tribe led by Chief Powhatan realized that the whites were a serious threat. They wanted more and more land, and every year more white settlers came over from Europe. Desperate, the Powhatan tribe launched a series of attacks, killing 347 colonists. It was not enough, however. The European settlers formed an army and drove the Powhatan off the coast of Virginia.

▼ Before the 1800s, Native American work in metal was rare, because almost no tribe developed the technique to extract metal from the earth. In the 1800s, however, southwestern craftsmen began learning how to work with silver, using techniques and styles perfected in Mexico, and they soon became experts.

This flower-bulb pattern is of squash blossoms, a common southwestern flower

The turquoise stone, with its colour of sky and water, was sacred to southwestern Native Americans

▼ This portrait of the Virgin Mary is over 300 years old and was painted by a Native American artist. It is evidence of the influence of the Spanish, who entered the American southwest in the 1600s and converted the native populations to Christianity. Christianity emphasized peace and love for one's neighbour, which matched pueblo beliefs.

The blue robe, the hands clasped in prayer, and the halo-like colours around Mary's head resemble details in European paintings of Mary at that time

Mixing cultures and artistic techniques

Like all artists who are influenced by meeting new people and new ways, Native American artists took materials, tools and techniques from the Europeans and made them their own. In the southwest, the pueblos introduced Christian symbols into some of their art. European glass beads were highly prized and became an important part of the designs on Lakota clothing. Navajo silver craftsmen started fashioning silver jewellery in the mid-1800s and used new types of dyes in their weaving. European metal tools were highly prized, and the enormous wooden totem poles of the northwest, carved with leering animals and humans and covered in bright European paints, only came into existence after the introduction of metal tools.

Clash of cultures

In the northeastern colonies, whites and Native Americans traded with each other. Beaver furs fetched high prices in Europe, and Native Americans exchanged **pelts** for guns, beads, metal pots and tools.

The settlers wanted more than just furs, however; they wanted land. In **New England**, the Native Americans watched with alarm as white settlers changed the landscape by building farms and towns. One Native American chief, King Philip, led a surprise attack on the New England colonies in 1675. Fifty-two of the region's 90 towns were attacked and 13 were destroyed. More than 600 settlers were killed. The English settlers reacted with fury and wiped out several Native American villages. Philip himself was killed in battle in 1676, and after the defeat, the Wampanoag tribe he had led was nearly wiped out.

Tecumseh

After the American War of Independence (1775–83), the USA looked westward to expand. They offered to buy land from the Native Americans. One tribal leader, a Shawnee named Tecumseh, urged his people to refuse. 'Sell a country!' he cried. 'Why not sell the air, the clouds, and the great sea? Did not the Great Spirit make them all for the use of his children?'

▲ A portrait of the Shawnee chief and warrior Tecumseh, leader of 15,000 warriors. Tecumseh tried to unite Native Americans to protect their land and lives from white settlers.

▼ A Cherokee *Primer* for school children dated 1845, printed in the Cherokee language.

The alphabet is still taught, learned and used by the Cherokee today

Greek, Hebrew and English letters were used as models for Cherokee letters

Cherokee Alphabet.

The five 'civilized' tribes

In the southeast, Native Americans adopted many white ways and married into white families. Five tribes – Creek, Cherokee, Choctaw, Chickasaw and Seminole – were called 'civilized' by many whites. The Cherokee laid out roads and built churches and schools. In 1821, a Cherokee silversmith named Sequoya finished writing an alphabet for the Cherokee language. Thousands of Cherokee learned to read. In 1828, the Cherokee acquired a printing press and published the first Native American newspaper, a bilingual Cherokee/English publication called the *Cherokee Phoenix*.

Tecumseh persuaded the tribes of the Ohio River Valley to join together against white settlers. Excited by Tecumseh's speeches, Native American warriors gathered at Tippecanoe in Indiana. But in 1811, while Tecumseh was away, a US army attack defeated the Native American force, and Tecumseh never regained his power. The Native American resistance broke into small groups, each too weak to resist the whites. Tecumseh continued his struggle but was killed in battle on 4 October 1813.

▼ *The Trail of Tears* painted by white American Robert Lindneux. In the 1830s, the tribes of the south were forced to leave their lands and travel west to barren reservations. Very few of the Native Americans rebelled, though some did flee to Canada or Mexico.

The Trail of Tears

In 1830, President Andrew Jackson signed the Indian Removal Act. This broke previous treaties. State governments seized the property of Native Americans. The surviving Native Americans were forced to sign new treaties that surrendered their land and began what became known as the 'Great Removal'.

From 1831 to 1839, about 50,000 southeastern Native Americans were herded to new lands further west, mostly in what is now Oklahoma. Many died from illness and lack of food. 'We were driven off like wolves,' remembered one, 'and our people's feet were bleeding with long marches. We are men. We have women and children, and why should we come like wild horses?' Native Americans remembered it as the 'Trail of Tears'.

Some had to carry what they owned on their backs

The movement was carried out under armed guard

People carried all of their possessions in wagons or strapped to animals

Losing the land

By the mid-1800s, Native Americans had been largely driven out of the eastern half of North America. White settlers kept moving west, travelling in creaking wagons over the **Plains** to reach the western states, especially after miners found gold in California in 1848.

Fort Laramie Treaty

Angered by the whites, bands of Native Americans attacked lone wagons and exploring parties. They raided homesteads. US **cavalry** units rode in pursuit, and fierce battles rocked the Plains. In 1851, most of the Native American tribes of the Plains agreed to a peace with the US government, signing a treaty at Fort Laramie. The treaty did not hold, however – mostly because whites could not stay out of Native American land.

Reservations

Rumours spread of gold on Native American land, and miners flocked there to dig for it. Again, angry Native American warriors killed many. In 1876, the army announced that all Native Americans had to report to a **reservation** or face war.

Many of them either did not hear the order, or they ignored it. Life on reservations was often bleak, harsh and with little opportunity. Many Native Americans were also oppressed culturally, forbidden to perform traditional ceremonies or wear traditional clothes. They compared living on a reservation to living in a cage. Thousands of Native Americans gathered that summer in a hunting camp, as they had for generations.

Women and children did not necessarily ride in the wagons; more often they walked alongside for most of the trip

▶ *A Wagon Train Heading West in the 1860s*, engraved by Stephane Pannemaker. During the mid-1800s, wagon trains carrying white settlers commonly crossed the Great Plains to Oregon and especially to California, where gold had been discovered. After 1870, however, more and more wagon trains settled in the **Mid-west**, leading to war with the Native American Plains tribes.

Oxen were the preferred animals to pull wagons because of their endurance and strength

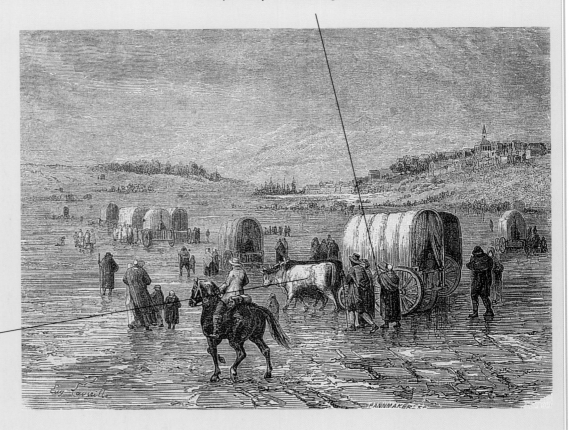

Battle of Little Bighorn

In June 1876, a US Army force was sent to find the camp, smash it, and drive the survivors on to reservations. But the campaign went wrong. One US unit was attacked and driven back. Another unit, under the command of George Armstrong Custer, brashly attacked the Native American camp on 26 June. Swarms of warriors surrounded half the unit, cut it off from the other half, and wiped it out. Custer was among the dead.

Stunned and enraged by their defeat, the whites relentlessly pursued Native American bands into the winter, broke up villages, and forced the survivors on to reservations. By this time, the giant buffalo herds were gone, slaughtered by white hunters. The Native American way of life on the Plains was ended.

▼ This drawing by an Oglala Sioux, Kicking Bear, depicts colourful columns of Native American warriors prepared for battle. Many of them carry a shield with an individual design, which was meant to grant the warrior protection in battle and victory over his enemies.

Sand Creek massacre

In 1864, a group of Cheyenne, part of a peace party travelling to **negotiate** a treaty with US soldiers, were attacked by whites while camped at Sand Creek, Colorado. The US force, numbering between 600 and 1000 men, were urged by their commander to 'kill and scalp all, big and little'. The chief, Black Kettle, frantically displayed American and white flags. The whites paid little attention, killing at least 200 men, women and children.

◄ Colonel John Chivington, known as the butcher of Sand Creek. Chivington was never prosecuted for the slaughter at Sand Creek, but widespread disgust forced his withdrawal from public life.

Native Americans did not typically use saddles, so the horses with saddles and no riders are almost certainly taken from the US Army

Each feather in a headdress represents a victory in battle

Some horses are also painted with designs meant to invoke the favour of spirits

Round shields were made from buffalo skin stretched over a frame and heated into a hard shell over a fire

Each shield is decorated with a unique design made by the warrior who carries it

Mound builders

The mound builders were part of a sophisticated civilization that flourished before Europeans appeared in North America. More than 3000 years ago, Native Americans in the central eastern woodlands buried their leaders in log-lined tombs constructed below ground. Gradually, they began heaping earth above the tombs – the first mound monuments. The custom spread to many Native American tribes in the east. Other mounds were constructed as elaborate temples. Many of these mounds survive, the faint outline of a ramp or staircase still visible.

▼ The Giant Serpent Mound in Adams County, Ohio, is one of the most impressive examples of earth art created by Native Americans. Why it was built, and what it was used for, is unknown, though it was probably the site of religious ceremonies.

The Giant Serpent Mound

From between 200 BC and AD 500, a Native American culture called the Hopewell constructed huge mounds, commonly in geometric shapes such as squares and circles. The most spectacular mound sculpture is of a writhing serpent, over 430 metres in length. The Giant Serpent Mound begins in a tight spiral, the body ripples and ends in open jaws about to consume what looks like an egg. Scholars are uncertain about exactly what the mound was designed for. Many believe the mound functioned as a ceremonial site for a group that worshipped a serpent spirit. In any case, the mound shows a sophisticated culture that could organize thousands of workers together to complete a major project.

This is thought to be an egg. The serpent's jaws are stretched open to swallow it

Average height of the mound is 1–2 m

The serpent mound is over 430 m in length

Other mound builders

The Hopewell were not the only Native American people that built mounds, and mound shapes vary a lot. There are conical tumuli (artificial hillocks), elongated or wall-like mounds, pyramidal mounds and effigy mounds (in the shape of animals). Between AD 1250 and 1400, a flat-topped mound at least 11 metres tall in Mississippi was the centre of rituals and trade. The top of the mound covered 3 hectares. The builders came from the Mississippi River valley.

However, there are limits to what modern researchers can deduce from ancient art, and the mound builders remind us of that. White settlers who first saw these mounds believed that a super race must have built them before Native Americans arrived on the continent. We do not know much about the mound builders. Clues to their civilization might have once existed in the form of skins or wooden structures, but any evidence of this kind disintegrated long ago in the moist climate. Scholars believe the mounds were mostly tombs, or had religious functions, as the site of temples or rituals.

History in landscape

The mound monuments give us tantalizing glimpses of ancient civilizations, but they also show evidence of a new one – the white civilization. Many of the mounds became part of farmland and many still show the grooves left by farmers with horse-drawn ploughs. Even the name Hopewell comes from the owner of the land where most of the sites were found.

▼ Many artefacts were buried in tombs and mounds. This shell artefact, probably a sort of brooch, was recovered from the Spiro Mound in Oklahoma.

This headdress and earrings are similar to those worn by Native Americans in Mexico

Badger or raccoon

The figures carry rattles, which were shaken during ceremonies to summon spirits

19

Traditional ways

Native Americans lived in groups of families called tribes, which shared a common language, history and tradition. Some tribes were large, numbering several thousand people, whereas others were made up of only a few hundred.

Many tribes broke up into smaller groups called bands during the winter. This made it easier to find food. In the summer, they came together in villages to hunt and plant crops in patches of cleared forest. Bound by family, culture and tradition, the tribe traded and waged war with other tribes and whites. Most tribes did not have a chief who ruled over them. It was only later, when Europeans insisted upon **negotiating** with a leader to trade goods, that chiefs became more common.

▼ This man performing outside a reconstructed Iroquois longhouse is a member of the False Face Society, a group who were healers. Later he will put on a mask and use tobacco, ashes and rattles to expel the source of a person's illness.

The rattle is commonly used in healing ceremonies to drive out illness

The longhouse is built from birch bark

▼ Tepee camp of the Crow tribe, Montana, photographed around 1900. A line of Crow horsemen ride through their camp.

The flaps at the top are open to allow smoke through

The ingenious structure of the tepee can be seen. It is made from buffalo skin stretched over a cone of poles

The riders are most likely a summer hunting party. Many of the men are shirtless in the heat

The League of Five Nations

One of the strongest political groups in North America was the Iroquois, who lived in the mountainous forests of what is today northern New York. They built long-houses up to 20 metres long out of wooden poles and bark. Some time in the mid-16th century, the Iroquois tribes came together in what they called the 'Great Peace'. They formed an alliance, the League of Five Nations, that stretched through upstate New York to Lake Erie. Every summer, the five Iroquois tribes sent representatives to discuss tribal matters. This council consisted of 50 members, and each tribe had one vote. The Iroquois political system was admired and respected by white **settlers**. It was later cited as an inspiration for the United States Constitution.

Leaders of the Lakota

The Lakota tribe was divided up into separate bands, each with its own chief, called an *itancan*. In the summer, these chiefs and their bands came together to form a tribal council. To be a chief of the band, a Lakota male had to have shown extraordinary bravery in battle, special magical powers, or great leadership ability. The leader of the largest band was usually recognized as the chief of the tribe.

The position as head chief was eagerly sought after, and the larger bands formed alliances with smaller bands to pick a leader. The bands occupied different spots in a vast circle at the summer encampment. The largest and most important band pitched their **tepees** opposite the entrance to the central **lodge**.

▶ Mother and child, photograph by Edward S. Curtis, c.1908.

The power of women

Some Native Americans societies were matrilineal, which means the family descent was followed through the mother's line. Among the Iroquois, the female head of the family, called a **clan** mother, held a strong position of influence in each **lodge**. When a man married a woman, he left his longhouse and joined hers. The clan mothers were powerful in tribal affairs. They held councils and elected the council of 50.

Nomads of the Plains

Some Native Americans made their home on the vast stretches of the Great **Plains**. They originally scratched a living through farming, hunting and gathering nuts and berries in the wooded areas along the Plains.

Horses

After European settlers arrived, bringing horses, the Plains way of life changed. Horses were greatly prized, as on horseback men could chase and kill many more buffalo than before.

▼ The paintings of George Catlin are an invaluable record of Native American life before extensive contact with white civilization changed them. Native Americans, especially on the Plains, were expert horse riders. This scene shows Native Americans chasing horses, and one horse being captured.

At first Native Americans bought or stole horses. Later they caught untamed ponies from the herds that had escaped from the settlers and had come to roam wild over the Great Plains. With horses, life was more secure and prosperous. Travel was quicker and easier. The size of Plains **tepees** grew larger.

These changes allowed more time for beautiful craftsmanship – beaded shirts and bags, feathered headdresses, and paintings of their exploits. To decorate clothing, craftsmen took porcupine quills, softened them in water, and pounded them flat. The quills were then dyed in various colours, producing a glossy sheen. The craftsmen used the quills to produce intricate patterns on dresses and bags. Later, craftsmen used glass beads which settlers traded with them. These designs were partly spiritual.

Clothes and decorations are of a young male warrior and the feathers record bravery and exploits in battle

Native Americans did not use leather reins and saddles on horses. They relied on simple ropes and blankets

Craftsmen of the Ponca tribe would deliberately place an odd coloured bead to break the pattern. The gesture was meant to keep them humble.

Recording deeds

On the Plains, circular shields were made from buffalo skin and painted. The paintings might be of visions and dreams seen by the individual warrior, and they gave the shield-bearer magical powers of protection. For example, an image of a buffalo head meant the owner would be as difficult to kill as the powerful buffalo.

Shields were often covered with graphic illustrations of battles, warriors carrying bows and arrows, spears and daggers, attacking each other in a swirl of figures. These images depicted the exploits of the warrior carrying the shield, inspiring awe and respect.

Native American men are typically shown wearing a war bonnet, although in fact it was worn only on the Plains. The bonnet was a spectacular trail of feathers fanning out above the wearer's head and down his back. It was most beautiful when fluttering in the wind, worn by a galloping rider.

▼ In 1832 George Catlin painted Four Bears, Chief of Missouri River Mandans, decorated in all his glory.

▶ This winter count reflects the growing presence of whites (the US soldier in blue uniform, and the flag) in Native American life.

Buffalo horns, to invoke the power, strength and importance of the buffalo

The spear was a typical weapon in hand-to-hand combat, rather than guns and bows and arrows

This feathered headdress, or war bonnet, represents the feats of bravery and honour of the entire tribe, not just the individual warrior

Winter count

A 'winter count' was a Native American way of recording history. The most important event of every year was painted in a tightening spiral. One winter count records the appearance of **smallpox**, by showing a figure covered with sores. Another year records a meteor shower with a circle and small crosses. The count also shows when the Native Americans were forced to abandon their tepees and live on **reservations**. Each year is marked with a log cabin.

Warfare

Native American tribes often clashed with each other. Confrontations provided chances to steal horses, expand **territory**, or prove one's bravery in battle. With the arrival of the Europeans, fighting occurred almost as soon as settlements were established. At Jamestown, Virginia, a clerk noted in 1610 that the settlers attacked a local Native American leader. 'Her town we burnt, and killed some of her people.'

Strength in numbers

Individually, Native American warriors were as brave and skilled in fighting as any European soldier. The whites, however, usually had more men, more guns and more supplies. They also fought more as a unit. They had a strict chain of command where soldiers followed the orders of officers. The Native Americans had war leaders, but they led primarily by example. Once the battle began, the Native American essentially fought alone, seeking individual honour.

The Native Americans did win several battles. In 1791, an US army of 1400 settlers was routed by 1200 Native Americans along the Wabash River, in what is today the state of Indiana. The Native American force, led by the Miami war chief Little Turtle, surprised the American force in a dawn attack and scattered the army. Despite such victories, however, the Native Americans could not win against the white civilization. There were simply too many settlers and too many soldiers with guns and horses.

▼ A Native American painting of a fight between two famous leaders, General Custer and Crazy Horse. This picture should not be considered historically accurate. Neither Crazy Horse nor General Custer looked like the figures drawn, and soldiers and Native Americans rarely fought each other on horses – they dismounted and fought on the ground.

US soldiers almost never carried swords in battle – they preferred guns

Carries a war club for close combat

The yellow stripe on his trousers shows he is from the cavalry

The Native American uses no saddle and guides the horse with a single strand of rope

Warfare on the Plains

The Plains Native Americans waged warfare for glory. The most esteemed feat of Plains warfare was 'counting coup'. A warrior counted coup by being the first to touch an enemy warrior, usually with a spear or lance. This was considered extremely brave, since it was far easier to shoot an opponent from a distance.

During the 1850s, 1860s and 1870s, Native American warriors adopted different tactics to defeat the white soldiers. Crazy Horse, a Lakota warrior, carried out an ambush that wiped out an 80-man US **cavalry** unit on 21 December 1866. Under Crazy Horse, the Native American warriors learned to fight more as a unit. Later, some US generals would call the Plains Native Americans the greatest force of light cavalry in the world. Yet the whites were still too strong. Worse, they waged war into the winter, killing ponies and burning villages, leaving the Plains Native Americans exposed to the bitter cold. Unable to protect or feed their families, the Plains Native Americans were forced to report to reservations.

▼ Iron Plume, a famous Sioux leader, was photographed in 1907 by Edward S. Curtis.

Objects of peace

The Iroquois did not have a written language, but one way they recorded important historical events was through **wampum** belts – belts on which pictures were stitched using tiny polished beads made from shells. They are a record of treaties among the tribes of the Iroquois Confederation, and of treaties with Europeans.

▼ A wampum belt. Wampum beads were made from sea shells and were highly prized, which made the belt an extremely valuable object. When whites arrived in North America, they quickly learned to use the wampum beads as currency. Many treaties with whites were recorded with wampum belts.

The string was made from the fibre of hemp, a plant

Wampum beads were made from the inside of clam shells

The pattern of beads represented a treaty

The beads were originally produced by Native Americans on Long Island, New York

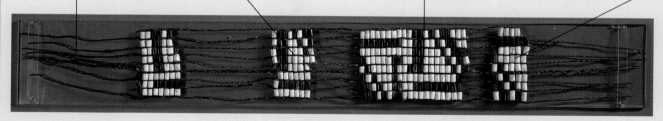

Buffalo robe painting

The Plains Native Americans were arguably the most advanced painters in North America. They used buffalo skins as their canvases, decorating objects such as shields, tepees, and especially robes.

Decorated buffalo robes were worn mostly on special occasions. The robes were covered with figures or designs that told that individual's story. The story might include encounters with spirits or ancestors.

▼ This dramatically painted robe shows Native American hunters chasing a giant buffalo herd, or individual episodes of a horseman encountering a buffalo. In the centre of the robe sits a chief on horseback, a tepee and important animal symbols. The painting indicates the importance of buffalo. The village stands in the centre of the robe, but it is the buffalo that fill the universe around it.

The painting on a buffalo robe might recount feats of bravery during warfare or hunting. Each robe, therefore, was and is unique.

Although one robe was always different from the next, Native Americans relied on similar imagery and style. Each animal had its own characteristics and strengths and weaknesses. Drawing a certain animal would be a gesture recognized throughout the tribe. People were also very aware of how battles and hunts were depicted. If someone tried to paint something on their robe that was not true or exaggerated their feats, he or she would be strongly condemned by the rest of the tribe.

Hunters are on horseback, though that happened only relatively recently in Native American history

Stripes of yellow and blue could have many meanings, including sunshine and night

The bird's brown and white feathers indicate it is most likely an eagle. The eagle was thought to be a messenger to the spirit world and was a symbol of great power

Buffalo skulls were used as decoration in many Great Plains villages as a gesture of respect

The tepee might represent a sacred space or a village

Several men, wearing feathers, dance or stand in some kind of formation – possibly a ceremony related to the hunt

In two instances a buffalo runs headlong at a hunter. This would be extremely unnerving and dangerous for the hunter

A scene from tribal life. A chief wears a long feathered headdress, a symbol of power, prestige and strength

▶ This painting shows a Native American painting a buffalo robe. The paintings would be a visual record of his feats and visions.

Animal hide used as canvas ———————

Native Americans commonly used painting tools made from spongy bone located in buffalo hips. The bone could soak up paint ———————

Men and women created different kinds of robes. The women decorated with highly abstract patterns and designs. Each shape and colour had a special meaning. In one robe, from the late 1800s, a Plains woman painted a rectangle in the centre, representing the earth. Two stripes, one red and one yellow, surrounded it – the yellow represented the sun, the red represented day. Another yellow stripe, this one running the length of the robe, evoked the Milky Way.

In contrast, robes painted by men were much more straightforward depictions of warriors and battles. Many of these drawings showed gruesome details, with hacked off limbs and showers of blood. When a great warrior wore such a robe in public it was a visible record of his bravery and inspired awe through the rest of the tribe.

Robes also depicted bravery during a hunt. Killing buffalo was no simple task and could often become very dangerous. A buffalo herd could stampede, trampling everything in its path. Or a buffalo might charge a man at a thundering gallop with its sharp

horns lowered. A wounded buffalo was perhaps the most dangerous and would attack anything that came too close.

Because each buffalo robe is unique, it is often difficult to understand exactly what the painter meant. Some images are easily recognized and understood. Others, however, are part of that individual's story, a private moment that had great meaning to that person, but unfortunately is lost to us today.

Sitting Bull

Sitting Bull was a famous chief of the Lakota. Quiet, intense and a keen observer, Sitting Bull urged the Lakota Sioux to maintain their way of life. He won his name as a teenager in battle with Crow warriors. It indicates the strength and endurance of the buffalo. Sitting Bull led the Lakota when they defeated Custer at the Battle of Little Bighorn. After the victory, Sitting Bull fled to Canada for several years and finally returned to a reservation. He was killed by Native American police in 1890, during a rebellion against white rule.

Everyday life

Hunting was essential to most Native American societies. Meat was a luxury. Animals were swift, could smell keenly, and were startled into flight at a slight sound. Against such formidable odds, Native Americans laboured to make deadly weapons and plotted hunting strategies. They worked together to trap deer, buffalo, fish and even whales.

Native American hunters honoured the spirit of the animal for giving up its life so that people could live. This belief gave rise to complex ceremonies and elaborate use of artwork. Some of the earliest Native American **artefacts** that have been found, some thousands of years old, were used to help the hunt. One is a model of an antelope made from twigs. Another is a graceful deer head carved from wood.

The Arctic Native Americans believed that they had to return animals to the spirit world to replenish the supply of **game**. To do this, they saved the bladder of every animal they killed. Each year, they held a bladder festival, in which inflated bladders of sea mammals were dropped into holes in the ice. The act was intended to return each animal's soul to the spirit world.

▼ White explorer George Catlin painted this scene in about 1832. It shows the Bison Dance of the Buffalo Society, a Mandan Plains hunting **ritual.** The buffalo was honoured as a powerful spirit and source of survival for the tribe.

The dance was meant to summon the sacred animals for a successful hunt

Dancers wear buffalo heads and tails that drape to their feet

They carry various weapons: spears, bows and arrows, and war clubs

▼ *Hunting Buffalo Camouflaged with Wolf Skins*, painted by George Catlin in about 1832.

Some buffalo start to take notice of the 'wolves'

A pair of Plains hunters approach a buffalo herd

Hunters are hidden under wolf skins to confuse or scare the herd

Hunting techniques

Native Americans employed elaborate ruses to trap animals. In the northeast, Penobscot hunters used deer masks to frighten herds of deer during an ambush. In the southeast, hunters sometimes disguised themselves in entire deerskins and were experts in imitating deer calls to lure prey closer.

On the Great **Plains**, hunters dressed in wolf or buffalo skins to confuse the buffalo herds and startle them into moving in a certain direction. When the herd was moving, some of the men jumped up, screaming and waving blankets. This terrified the buffalo, which began to stampede. The hunters guided them over a cliff, where they either died from the fall or from volleys of arrows.

Hunting rituals and masks

Hunters used to disguise themselves with masks and furs. Clad in these items, they could sneak up on their prey. Later, the masks and furs were used in hunting ceremonies for spiritual reasons.

Not for fun or sport

Hunting was never done for fun or sport. The animal provided many vital items, not just food. Native Americans used almost every piece of the buffalo. Buffalo meat provided food. Needles and axes were fashioned from bones. The skin was stitched into clothing or draped over poles to make **tepees**. The horns were boiled into glue and the blood used as paint. The wispy tail was perfect to shoo away flies. Native American tribes made similar use of other animals they hunted: elk, moose, rabbits, deer, even walrus.

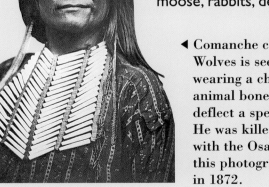

◀ Comanche chief Heap Wolves is seen proudly wearing a chest mantle of animal bones, as armour to deflect a spear or arrow. He was killed in combat with the Osage shortly after this photograph was taken in 1872.

Resources of nature

Native American art was heavily influenced by each tribe's environment. People drew from the local landscape for materials. In the northeast, they took **wampum** beads from the seashore and wove them into belts. In the southwest, they used vegetables to dye their rugs and blankets. On the Plains, people used buffalo hides in almost every work of art they produced. In the northwest, the cedar pine trees provided wood that was both strong and easy to carve, and they used it to create masterpieces.

Trees

In the northeast, Native Americans used bark from the area's many birch trees. The bark was supple and strong, and people cut it and stitched it together with spruce root to make boxes. Because the bark was plentiful, these tribes made very few baskets and no pottery. Bark was also used to build canoes.

▼ This painting, made by Paul Kane in 1845, shows a Native American camp on Lake Huron.

Dogs were popular in camps. They were loyal and they could carry some goods

Canoes, essential for travel and fishing, were made from bark

Tepees were made from bark

30

In the thickly forested northwest, the giant red cedar tree formed the basis of the culture's art and architecture. People lived in rectangular wooden **lodges**, each one housing several families. The lodges were built from a cedar wood frame covered by cedar planks. Outside each lodge was a totem pole, carved from a giant tree trunk. Mats made from the bark were hung on lodge walls. Roots were woven into baskets.

The long beak identifies this bird on the handle as a raven

Other materials

To fashion utensils and dishes, the northwestern Native Americans turned to local mountain goats. A goat's horn was softened in boiling water, then craftsmen straightened it and cut out a piece that was then carved and shaped into a bowl, a spoon, or a ladle.

In the dry and hot southwest, Native American builders used the sun to make effective building materials.

▶ Finely carved ladles were used in important feasts held during the winter season. This ladle from the late 19th century shows how intricately the northwestern Tlingit people used to decorate many of their objects.

Decorated with copper and abalone shell

The ladle is made from goat or sheep horn softened in boiling water and then shaped

The importance of trade

Sometimes, the Native Americans could not find everything they wanted locally. They readily traded with other tribes and whites. **Wampum** beads were in great demand throughout the northeast and even served as a **currency**. The Plains Native Americans could not find many porcupines on the Plains, so they traded for quills with Native Americans in the north and east.

▶ This bag is made from flattened porcupine quills, deer hair and skin from a mallard (duck). Each person decorated things as they wished, though the patterns and shapes usually followed examples set by other tribal craftsmen.

They laid out slabs of a mud mixture that dried and hardened, and was known as **adobe**. The adobe bricks were stacked and covered with a muddy paste. The bricks were strong enough to support the construction of large buildings, which formed the **pueblos**. Many of these pueblos, some more than 1000 years old, can still be seen and visited.

To make pottery, pueblo artists dug different coloured clay from the landscape and moulded it into jars. Pottery was sacred in the pueblos. In the Santa Clara Pueblo, for example, the same word was used for pottery, *nung*, as for people. This reflected the belief that people, just like pots, were formed from the sacred earth.

Hair and decoration

Native Americans loved elaborate decoration and pomp, especially in their clothing, jewellery and hair. This was never, however, just about vanity or for display. Every item, colour and decoration made an important point, usually about rank or a stage of life.

Feather decoration

The Plains people often wore feathers in their hair or bonnets. Each feather meant something different. An upright feather with a small strip of horsehair indicated a coup in battle. A red feather with bands showed the wearer was wounded but that he had also killed enemies – one band per kill. A feather with a red dot indicated the wearer had killed a foe. Feathers were a visual display of a warrior's feats in combat. In battle, great warriors often sought each other out according to the feathers they wore.

Hair

Native Americans rarely grew beards or moustaches, but plucked out hairs with shell, wooden tweezers, or bone. The hair on their head, however, was prized by both male and female Native Americans. A hairstyle could tell an important fact about the wearer. Hopi girls of marriageable age wore their hair in the shape of a squash blossom (a squash is a pumpkin-type vegetable). Before they were allowed to wear this style of hair, they had to perform several difficult tasks, including grinding corn for four days. Once the girl had showed her skill, she could wear the squash blossom hairstyle.

▼ An Osage warrior painted by Saint-Memin in around 1800. Most Native Americans enjoyed jewellery, paint and elaborate hairstyles. The decorations were important indicators of a person's status.

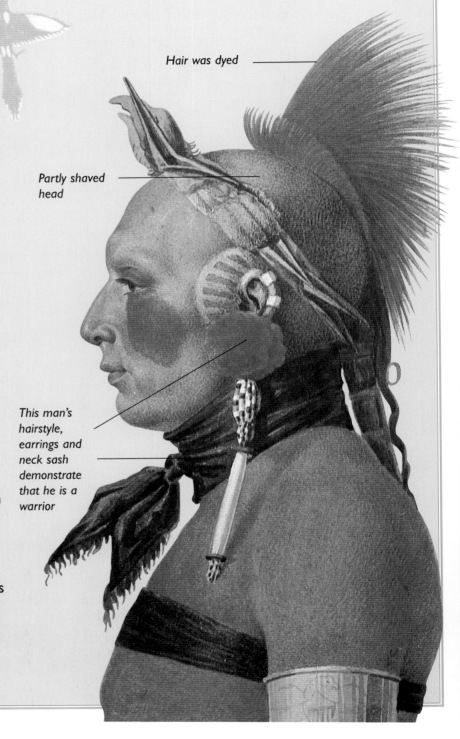

Hair was dyed

Partly shaved head

This man's hairstyle, earrings and neck sash demonstrate that he is a warrior

Other Native American tribes devoted similar attention to their hair. Some shaved most of their scalp and let one lock grow out. They mixed bear fat with pigments to dye it a special colour. They styled it and wore it in braids. In the late 1800s, men and boys living on **reservations** were forced to cut their hair. This was a devastating blow, since the men took great pride in their hair. In the early 1900s, they resorted to wearing long-haired wigs made out of horsehair.

Magical clothing

Some clothing was considered so powerful that it could give the wearer protection in battle. In the late 1880s, the Arapaho Native Americans stitched shirts with designs for a ceremony called the Ghost Dance, believing that their lost way of life would be restored to them. The shirt, they were sure, would protect them from the white man's bullets. Tragically, they were wrong, and many Native Americans were massacred at Wounded Knee on 29 December 1890.

▶ An Arapaho Ghost Dance dress with painted design of birds, turtle and stars. Prophets proclaimed that the Ghost Dance would rid the land of white people and restore the old ways.

The bird images are most likely of Thunderbird, a mythical animal known in many Native American cultures. When it beat its wings, it caused thunder; when it opened its eyes, it flashed lightning. By covering a robe with images of Thunderbird, the wearer hoped to gain its power and strength

Jewellery

The wearing of beautiful items was very important to many Native American tribes. In the northeast, where some tribes had access to shells, especially wampum, shell jewellery was worn. Jewellery was more than just an object of beauty. A special pendant or design could indicate the rank and the **clan** of the wearer.

Stars and moon design represents the heavens

Dress is made of buckskin

*In many **Creation stories,** the Earth was created on a turtle's back*

Family life

Most Native Americans lived in extended families called clans. Several clans, or bands, made up a tribe. Work roles were usually separated by sex. The women traditionally prepared and cooked food and tended to the crops in the fields. The men largely hunted and waged war.

Childhood

European observers wrote that the Native Americans expressed great love for their children and were rarely strict with them. The Native Americans taught by example and stories, rather than with punishment. Native American children, however, were expected to be obedient and serious about relations with other tribal members, and about the life and death struggles of the hunt or battle.

Native American children enjoyed playing with toys made especially for them. They had dolls, complete with flowing buffalo hair and beaded dresses as beautiful as real dresses. There were horses and riders. The dolls even sometimes had a place to live in – a fully painted miniature tepee. Children from the pueblos were given **kachina** dolls, carved from the roots of a cottonwood tree, to play with. But these were not simply toys. Kachinas are supernatural beings representing the dead, forces of nature or local features such as springs. Kachina dolls were used to teach children about pueblo spiritual beliefs and to discipline unruly children. Bad children might be confronted by an angry kachina with a yucca whip.

▶ Kachina dolls were given to Hopi children. There are several hundred different kachinas.

Clothes made of leather

Buffalo, or cow, headdress

A lightning bolt was a good sign to southwestern Native Americans – it meant rain for their crops

Rattles were important parts of ceremonies

Basic doll is made of wood

At the age of eight or nine, boys were taken into the **kiva** (an underground chamber regarded as sacred space) and surrounded by people dressed as kachinas with whips. Each boy received four lashes. They were then given gifts of corn meal and feathers. After a celebratory meal, the kachinas removed their masks and showed themselves to be men of the village. These young boys had been initiated into (or shown for the first time) the ceremonies of pueblo life.

Courtship

Native Americans, like people everywhere, had rules and customs for falling in love and finding a mate. On the Plains, there was rarely any private space for a young couple to talk. When a young man and woman fell in love, they had to conduct a courtship in the open. Unable to speak directly to a young girl, a young man might sing a love song nearby. If she found him attractive, then she might invite him to stand with her wrapped in a blanket. The two could then speak to each other intimately, perhaps planning for a common future. This was called 'blanket courting'.

The slender drawn columns on the headboard above the mask are meant to represent corncobs and fertility

Pine boughs represent vegetation, the green of the earth

▶ This masked dancer is a corn kachina. Corn was extremely important to people in the southwest. This kachina's participation in the ceremony was meant to bring rain and guarantee a successful crop.

Potlatches

Northwestern Native Americans were very concerned with **status**. Chiefs were expected to give 'potlatches', ceremonies with a lavish banquet. It was an occasion for the chief to show his wealth and his generosity. Each potlatch ended with the elaborate handing out of gifts to each person. Everyone observed closely: the chief could not appear greedy or poor.

◀ This painting, by Frederick Remington in 1892, shows a group sitting in their lodge during a potlatch ceremony. The purpose and customs of the potlatch were different for each tribe and could take years to plan. Each gift had to be carefully chosen and was presented elaborately with a story.

Beliefs and mythology

Native American nations were very different, but they all believed that the world was sacred and that everything in it possessed a spirit. Stories played an important role in explaining the order and origin of the world, how humans were made, and the roles of animals, weather and people.

The Native American cultures believed in a 'Great Spirit' that ruled over the universe. The northeastern Algonquin called it Gitchi Manitou; the **Plains** Lakota called it Wakan Tanka. The Great Spirit is usually not defined further, but it gives birth and purpose to other beings and spirits.

Creation myth

Many Native American **Creation stories** use the same elements. In the Cheyenne Creation myth, the universe is a giant ocean filled with fish, with birds flying overhead. The birds grow exhausted and seek a place to rest. To find earth, they dive to the bottom of the sea. Only one bird is able to scoop up a ball of mud and return to the surface. The mud expands and becomes land. It grows larger and eventually the turtle can carry it on its back. Many of the creation stories have a different animal that dives to the bottom of the ocean, but the turtle is almost always the animal which carries the earth. Many tribes called the land around them 'turtle island'.

▼This shield was decorated by a Cheyenne warrior during the 1860s, a time when Plains people were under pressure from white settlers. Warriors carried shields like this one into battle.

Shield is covered with things, especially feathers

Images of birds are most likely included for the powers the bird represents. The warrior would rely on these powers when fighting in battle

Design was painted by the owner of the shield according to his individual vision

Feathers were a common symbol of bravery on the Great Plains

Depicting deeds in art

The Native American peoples did not have a written language; they were largely oral cultures. This means they told stories that were passed down from one generation to the next. These stories were also expressed in art.

In the northwest, the complex carvings on totem poles and other wooden objects told family stories or showed lineage, such as how the family had received some power or right from an ancestor. This ancestor may have met an animal, shared adventures with it, and been rewarded.

On the Plains, individuals used art to tell their own stories. Lakota men painted exploits of the hunt and war on their **tepees**. Only a warrior who had earned great honour and respect could do this. Warriors also painted their shields. The Crow, who lived near the Lakota, often decorated their shields with feathers and drawings of Thunderbird. Thunderbird was an extremely powerful mythological beast, and anyone who painted it on his shield hoped that the creature's power would aid him in battle. Shields also carried other designs, usually things very personal to whoever carried the shield. They might be visions the warrior experienced.

▼ This scene of combat was painted on a tepee by Mandan Chief Mato-Tope in the 1830s. It probably depicts one of his victories over an opponent.

Flint-lock pistol firing — Mato-Tope often drew guns firing to create a war-like atmosphere in his drawings

One is cutting off the arm of the other with a hatchet

Body paint

Myths were not just important to cultures, but also to individuals. Each Native American, through visions and dreams, developed a myth for him or herself. Warriors and **shamans** all experienced contact with the spirit world in the form of visions. They later used these visions to decorate their bodies with paint, especially before important **rituals** and battle.

Totem poles

Seven tribes lived along the rocky and wooded coast that stretched from Oregon to Alaska. In the summer, they made their homes in rows of wooden houses erected on beaches. On one side lay the cold, misty ocean; on the other were dense forests of towering evergreen cedar trees.

The ocean provided food. The Native Americans collected baskets of shellfish, and speared seals for their fur. They threw nets across streams that filled with salmon each year. Having this reliable food source was a luxury inland tribes did not have. It allowed the northwestern Native Americans the time and energy to carve totem poles. Cedar trees provided wood that was both massive and easy to carve, and Native American artists created giant totem poles with carvings of animals, people and spirits.

A symbol of prestige

Totem poles varied in size. Some stood 3 metres tall, while others reached more than 20 metres. The best poles are spectacular examples of carving: snarling grizzly bears, eagles and killer whales. The poles were not just for decoration. They showed the animal crest of the family and told the family's history in legends.

▼ Reconstruction of a typical northwestern Native American seashore village. The animals carved on the totem pole were considered to be the **clan**'s ancestors, that would help members of the clan when they needed them.

Probably a memorial pole erected by the chief of the village to show his authority and powers. It was especially tall so it could be seen by anyone approaching in a canoe from the ocean

This totem pole is most likely a 'portal pole'. In the pole was a doorway into the longhouse. Entering the longhouse represented passing into a new world

This is probably a raven (a hero or trickster common in northwestern myths)

A grizzly bear

A typical legend would explain how a family's ancestors met an animal in the forest and spoke with it. The ancestor and the animal went through many adventures together and the animal gave the ancestor and his family the right to hunt in its **territory**. To symbolize this agreement, the ancestor returned to the village and adopted the animal as his crest. The crest gave the family hunting and fishing privileges, which were extremely important in northwest society. The poles were meant to show a family's power and wealth, and they were tall enough to be visible from the ocean. Many of the poles were painted in bright colours to add effect. Totem poles tell us about a society that thought it was important to express each family's **status**.

Lost to the elements

Unfortunately, the wood that totem poles are carved from does not withstand the northwestern wind, cold and moisture. Not many poles survive more than 100 years. Many have been preserved in museums, but they do not have the same impact in a museum as when they rise up over a beach. They are a symbol of pride, a bold statement of a family's identity.

▶ A totem belonging to the Kwakiutl tribe. Different totem poles were erected for different purposes. Some were placed in front of cemeteries to honour the dead, others were mounted in front of homes to show the owner's ancestry. This pole shows two beasts that were feared and revered by northwestern Native Americans: Thunderbird and the grizzly bear.

Thunderbird

One of the most common images in northwestern art is of Thunderbird. Thunderbird is the powerful spirit of the sky. The beating of its massive wings generates thunderclaps, its eyes and beak flash lightning. Thunderbird soars over the ocean and feeds upon whales, which it hoists from the sea in its talons. The **lodges** and totem poles of the northwest often show Thunderbird, its wings outstretched and its feet gripping a whale.

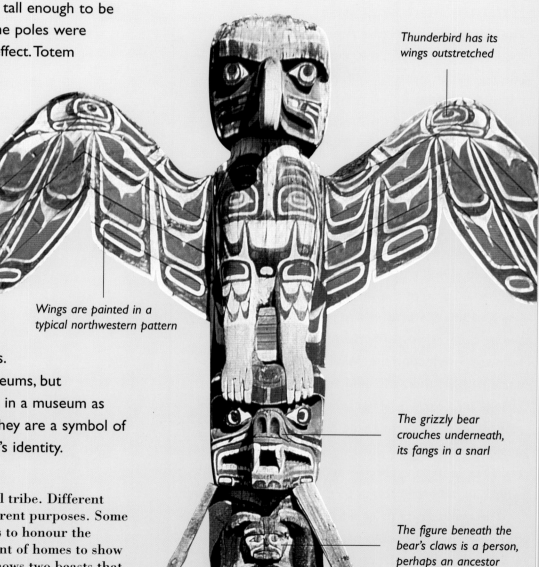

Thunderbird has its wings outstretched

Wings are painted in a typical northwestern pattern

The grizzly bear crouches underneath, its fangs in a snarl

The figure beneath the bear's claws is a person, perhaps an ancestor

Masks

Most Native American cultures made some kind of mask. Masks were (and are) an essential part of religious and cultural ceremonies. They have fantastic, wildly imaginative designs and are some of the finest art Native Americans ever produced.

Rituals and legends

The northwestern Native Americans spent their summers fishing, trapping and hunting. When winter came, with its cold mists, the people stayed close to home, where they survived on stocks of food. During this time the tribes re-enacted legends and performed **rituals** in the dim light of campfires. Artists were essential to these rituals. They carved and decorated elaborate masks to shock and excite the audience. Some of the masks were technical wonders that swung open to reveal human faces beneath – reflecting the belief that in ancient times men and animals could change into each other at will. Other masks had mouthpieces that could be changed, designed to produce different sound effects and voices. Features such as eyebrows and lips were moveable, which added great drama to the delivery of a speech.

The tradition of using masks extended all the way to Alaska, where people produced some of the most vivid, distorted and fantastic masks ever. They are designed to show both the surface of an object (animal or mythological creature) and its inner soul at the same time. The Iroquois, in the northeast, carved highly stylized masks that were used in ceremonies. They carved the masks out of live trees, believing that was the way to preserve the tree's spirit in the mask.

▼ A mid-19th-century Kwakiutl mask. Masks were intended to be spirits and magical animals. This mask would look quite frightening as it appeared out of the darkness into the flickering light of a fire.

Mask is carved from wood

Human hair

Painted face was supposed to startle the audience

Kachinas

In the **pueblos** of the southwest, Native American mythology is populated by hundreds of spirits called **kachinas**. There is a kachina spirit for virtually everything – rain, clouds, the dead, gods and goddesses. In ceremonies, a member of the tribe will wear a kachina mask that allows the wearer to become the spirit. Some kachinas bring medicine and healing powers, some control the seasons, others bless new homes. Kachina dolls are both works of art and important teaching tools, to help young people learn the hundreds of complex stories of the kachina spirits.

In dances and ceremonies in darkened **kivas**, people wearing masks played the part of kachina spirits. The mask allowed the wearer to transform himself into the spirit he represented. The mask was not simply a cover for a face. It brought the spirit world into the Native Americans' world, and by bringing these worlds together they ensured the health and success of the tribe.

▼The ruins of a kiva. This round chamber would have been a complete stone wall circle covered with logs and earth to shut out all light.

The kiva

When people in the southwest started to build multi-storey homes above the ground, they did not forget the underground chambers they used to live in. These dark chambers became sacred spaces, known as kivas, used for gatherings of societies or religious ceremonies. They provided the perfect stage for a masked kachina dancer.

▼This painting shows a variety of kachina spirits. Each kachina spirit was different and was decorated with different items, which the person wearing them could often choose.

This is most likely a 'mudhead', a type of clown

The figures at both ends of the line wear elaborate feather decorations

41

Spirits and shamans

Shamans acted as go-betweens for this world and the spirit world. Shamans were believed to have had direct contact with a spirit. This meeting became the shaman's original myth, a story that explained how he received his power.

▼ Shaman or medicine man of the Piegan tribe holding a sacred pipe, which played a central role in ceremonies.

He has traditional long, plaited hair

Pipe is elaborately decorated with feathers

Shamans

Shamans are often called medicine men. Many shamans were very knowledgeable about how different plants and roots could cure disease and injuries. Shamans, however, did not just treat a sick body. They sought to heal the spirit as well. These cures required rituals, songs, prayers and chants.

Shamans among the northwestern peoples grew into very powerful figures. When the shaman died, his body was not cremated as other bodies were. Instead, he was buried in a spot he had selected. His grave was treated with great respect and fear. When Native Americans passed by, they turned their faces and tossed offerings to avoid disapproval.

A bridge to the spirit world

Helped by aids such as tobacco, shamans could go into trances and speak with the dead. Shamans also relied on special objects to perform their tasks. Medicine men from the northwest used rattles carved from wood and filled with pebbles. The sound of the rattle was believed to stimulate spiritual forces and bring the person more into balance with the world around them. Animals associated with magic, the otter for example, were often depicted on the rattle.

Pipes

Throughout Native American culture, smoking pipes was often considered a sacred ritual. Smoking was believed to bring a spiritual dimension to any meeting. Pipes were therefore carved into elaborate designs and were decorated with symbols. Often, these decorations, such as feathers or fur, were personal to the owner of the pipe.

A sling

Several charms are on his bow: a rabbit and three bird feathers

A bow

◀ A 19th-century painting of a shaman. A shaman had the power to communicate with the spirit world.

Vision quest

Many Native Americans went on vision quests, which usually involved fasting and travelling to a remote, secluded place. The man hoped to have contact with his spiritual guardian, who usually appeared as an animal, or as one of the elements. In this meeting, the spirit passed on valuable information to the individual, who used it for the rest of his life as inspiration and protection.

Sand paintings

Sand paintings, primarily found in the southwest, were a pattern of earth and stone on a bed of sand. Most sand paintings depicted spirits, gods or sacred spots. Shamans created the paintings as part of religious ceremonies to heal, and more than 600 designs have been recorded. After the ceremony, the sand painting was swept away.

▲ A Navajo sand painting. Sand paintings were made out of different coloured sand and earth for ceremonies, especially healing rituals.

Bags used to carry ceremonial items were also decorated with potent symbols that showed their importance and gave them magical qualities. A bag woven in Wisconsin shows the dark profile and long tail of a mythical panther that people believed roamed the countryside.

Timeline

60,000 BC to 8000 BC
people migrate from Asia to North America, either over a land bridge between Alaska and Russia, or in boats

300 BC – AD 700
Hopewell culture flourishes in the eastern woodlands

AD 900
Hohokum people begin irrigating farmland

1200
mounds are constructed in Alabama

1300
large **pueblo** communities are abandoned

1492
Christopher Columbus, searching for a shorter route to the Indies, lands in North America. He calls the inhabitants 'Indians'

1596
Spanish explorers establish missions among the pueblo villages

1607
English establish a colony at Jamestown, Virginia

1620
Pilgrims on the *Mayflower* land in Massachusetts

1622
Powhatan Wars begin between Virginian Native Americans and English **settlers**

1636–37
Pequot War in New England. Pequot villages are destroyed by white settlers

1675–76
King Philip's War is waged in the northeastern colonies

1680
people of the pueblos rebel against Spanish rulers

1689
Spanish begin the re-conquest of pueblos

1729
French destroy the Natchez tribe

1754–63
French and Indian War results in defeat of the French. French colonies in North America are taken over by the English

1783
US government issues a proclamation that whites cannot settle on Native American land without permission or a treaty

1790–91
Native Americans resist white settlers entering the Ohio River Valley

1803
US government buys most of central North America from France. The 'Louisiana Purchase' doubles the size of the USA

1811
Native Americans are defeated at the Battle of Tippecanoe

1813
Tecumseh is killed in battle

1830
President Andrew Jackson signs the Indian Removal Act. Thousands of Native Americans are forced from their homes in the southeast. The forced migration is usually remembered as the 'Trail of Tears'

1830

influenza kills thousands of Native Americans in California and Oregon

1837

smallpox sweeps through tribes in the Missouri region

1846–48

USA defeats Mexico in the Mexican War and seizes **territory** from Texas to California

1848–49

gold is reported in California. The 'Gold Rush' brings millions of whites to the west coast

1850–60

cholera epidemic devastates tribes in the **Mid-west**

1851

Fort Laramie Treaty is signed

1853–56

USA signs dozens of treaties with Native Americans that give them more than 70 million hectares of land. Virtually all the treaties are eventually broken

1862

smallpox devastates the northwestern Native American tribes

1864

Sand Creek massacre

1865

second Fort Laramie Treaty is signed

1866–68

Plains Native Americans successfully resist the building of a road – the Bozeman Trail – into their land

1870s

buffalo are slaughtered in enormous numbers by white hunters

1876

Battle of Little Bighorn results in defeat for the 7th **Cavalry**

1877

surviving Plains Native Americans are pursued and forced onto **reservations**

1890

Ghost Dance movement inspires Native Americans to believe that they will rise against the whites and reclaim their way of life. At Wounded Knee Creek, 200 Native Americans preparing for the Ghost Dance are killed by US troops

1924

in recognition of Native American service in World War I, all Native Americans are declared US citizens

1960s

new consciousness (awareness) is raised among Native Americans, who either continue their artistic traditions or rediscover old ones

1973

members of the American Indian Movement occupy the Wounded Knee massacre site for 71 days to protest against white policies. Two Native Americans are killed before the siege ends

1991

Native American population is declared at 1,959,234 by the US Census Bureau, a 40 per cent increase on the figures for 1980

Glossary

adobe sun-dried mud bricks

arid parched, too dry for vegetation to thrive

artefact product made by humans

cavalry armed unit mounted on horses

clan family, in which descent is traced through only the male or only the female line. Most Native American clans are matrilineal – that is, they are traced through, and belong to, their mother's clan

Creation story story that tries to explain how the world was made

extinct obsolete. A species or culture that has died out

game wild animals that are hunted for food or sport

kachina ancestral spirit of the pueblo people; masked dancer representing a spirit; doll dressed as a particular spirit

kiva underground chamber in a pueblo village, used for ceremonies or councils

lodge Native American dwelling, such as a wooden house, or wigwam; the group living in such a dwelling

Mid-west region of north central USA around the Great Lakes and the upper Mississippi Valley

negotiate discuss and try to resolve an issue

New England region of northeastern USA, comprising the modern-day states of Maine, New Hampshire, Vermont, Massachusetts, Connecticut and Rhode Island

nomadic moving from one place to another; not staying in one spot for long

pelt skin of an animal, with the fur still on it

Plains (or Great Plains) a vast region of gently rolling grassland in central North America. The climate can be blazing hot in summer, bitterly cold in winter

pueblo Native American village of the southwest, with buildings of adobe brick

reservation area of land set aside for Native Americans to live on by the US government at the end of the 19th century

ritual special words and actions used at a ceremony, maybe a religious ceremony

settlers people coming to live in a new land. In the 19th century millions of settlers arrived in North America from Europe, hoping to make new lives for themselves

shaman someone who acts as a medium between the material world and the spirit world, who practises magic or sorcery for healing, foretelling the future and claiming control over natural events

smallpox highly infectious, often deadly disease, giving a high fever and spots

status person's position in society

tepee portable, cone-shaped tent made of buffalo hide with a framework of poles, used on the Plains

territory land traditionally, or legally, lived on and used by a group of people

wampum small beads made from polished shells, used by certain Native American peoples as currency, jewellery or for ceremonial exchanges between groups

Further resources

Books

Berlo, Janet Catherine, *Oxford History of Art: Native North American Art* (Oxford University Press, 1998)

Ferguson, Diana, *Native American Myths* (Collins & Brown, 2001)

Hook, Jason, *People Who Made History: Native Americans* (Wayland, 2000)

Hull, Robert, *Native North American Stories* (Wayland, 1992)

Macdonald, Fiona, *Plains Indians* (Oxford University Press, 1992)

Reynoldson, Fiona, *Living Through History: Native Americans* (Heinemann Library, 2000)

Rossi, Renzo, *The Atlas of Human History: Civilizations of the Americas: Native American Cultures of North, Central and South America* (Cherrytree Books, 1996)

Thomson, Ruth, *Young Craft Topics: Indians of the Plains* (Franklin Watts, 1991)

Websites

http:www.kidinfo.com/American_History/Native_Americans.html
Kid Info – reference resources on Native Americans

cybersleuth-kids.com/sleuth/History/Native_Americans/Index.htm
The Native American history section of an information site for children

http://americanhistory.si.edu/timeline/01pots.htm
National Museum of American History – information on and photos of pottery styles

http://www.conexus.si.edu/map/exhibit.htm
National Museum of the American Indian Exhibits Online – exhibits of art from the Smithsonian Museum

http://www.si.edu/resource/faq/nmai/start.htm
Smithsonian Institution: Native American Resources – describes the collections that relate to Native Americans

Index

Titles in the *History in Art* series include:

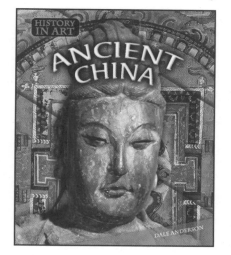

Hardback   1 844 43369 2

Hardback   1 844 43361 7

Hardback   1 844 43359 5

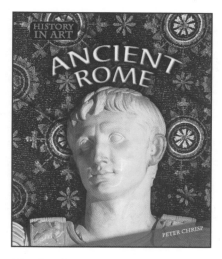

Hardback   1 844 43360 9

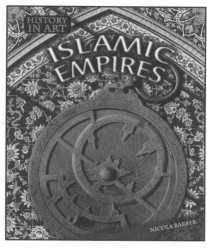

Hardback   1 844 43362 5

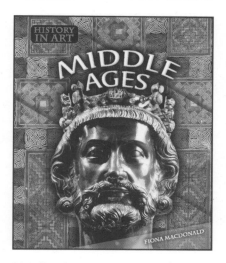

Hardback   1 844 43370 6

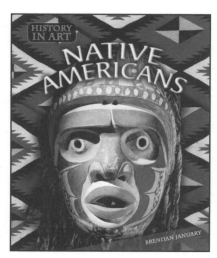

Hardback   1 844 43371 4

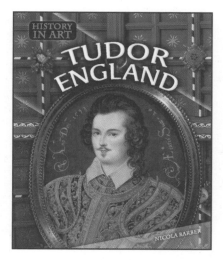

Hardback   1 844 43372 2

Hardback   1 844 43373 0

Find out about the other titles in this series on our website www.raintreepublishers.co.uk